Amazing Facts
from
THE
BIBLE

A children's fun book
of knowledge

**BETSY ROSSEN ELLIOT
and J. STEPHEN LANG
Illustrated by
S.D. SCHINDLER**

JOSHUA MORRIS PUBLISHING

British Library Cataloguing-in-Publication Data.
A catalogue record for this book is available from
the British Library

ISBN 1-85724-832-5

Printed in Hong Kong.

CONTENTS

And, if you're still wondering about those questions on the cover:

Noah's ark was about 136 metres long, 23 metres wide, and 13 metres high—about as big as an airship! (Genesis 6:15)

Goliath was over 270 cm tall! (1 Samuel 17:4-7)

King Solomon, hailed as the wisest king of Israel, taught people about plants, animals, birds, snakes, and fish. (1 Kings 4:33)

The first musician was Jubal, who invented the harp and flute. (Genesis 4:21)

The first twins were Jacob and Esau, the sons of Isaac and Rebekah and the grandsons of Abraham. (Genesis 25:19-24)

PEOPLE IN THE BIBLE

What famous king lived in the wilderness and ate grass?

King Nebuchadnezzar was chased from his palace, and for seven years he lived with the animals in the field and ate grass like the cows—just as the prophet Daniel predicted. (Daniel 4:19-33)

Who were the Nazirites?

They were a group of men and women in Israel who were especially devoted to God's service. (Numbers 6:1-2)

What was one of the special vows the Nazirites took?

Each Nazirite promised that he would never cut his hair, but when he became a member of the group he had to shave his head! (Numbers 6:5, 18-19)

8

Which pair of brothers were the first farmer and shepherd?
Cain and Abel, the sons of Adam and Eve, were the first to till the soil and take care of sheep. (Genesis 4:2)

What did Absalom do only once a year?
Cut his hair—but only when it got too heavy to carry around. This grew to be a big problem though (see *The Natural World*, page 50). (2 Samuel 14:25-26)

What did the men of Israel do when they were in mourning?
They would either cut off their beards or pull out the hairs with their hands. (Ezra 9:3)

9

What unusual souvenir from Israel did Naaman take back home to Syria?
Earth! The army commander was so thankful that God cured him of a skin disease called leprosy that he carried earth from Israel back to Syria so he could worship God on the same ground. (2 Kings 5:14-17)

Some people like to collect stamps. What interesting hobby did King Mesha of Moab have?
He took care of sheep.
(2 Kings 3:4)

Who was shipwrecked and spent a whole day and night floating on the open sea?
The apostle Paul—and that was only one of the three times he was shipwrecked! (2 Corinthians 11:25)

10

Who became a mother at the age of 90?
Sarah, wife of Abraham, was 90 when her son, Isaac, was born.
(Genesis 17:17, 21:1-2)

Which doctor wrote two books in the New Testament?
Luke wrote the Gospel with his name and the Book of Acts, which he wrote while travelling with Paul. Luke wrote both books for his friend Theophilus.

Elizabeth and Mary were relatives and were pregnant at the same time. What surprising thing happened when Mary (Jesus' mother) came for a visit?
The baby inside Elizabeth—who became known as John the Baptist when he grew up—jumped when he heard Mary's voice. (Luke 1:35-45)

11

Who was the greatest songwriter in the Bible?
That honour probably goes to King Solomon.
Besides his other great achievements, he wrote
over a thousand songs. (1 Kings 4:32)

Which king was also a fine musician?
David was known as the "sweet singer
of Israel." He wrote 73 of the psalms
in the Bible, and once hired 4,000
musicians to play in praise of the Lord
on instruments he had made himself!
(1 Chronicles 23:5)

12

Who was the first cheerleader?

Moses. As long as he held his rod up, the Israelites were winning their fight with the Amalekites. When his arms got tired, Aaron and Hur stood by Moses to hold his arms up. (Exodus 17:11-13, TLB)

What was a fuller?

People who laundered clothes in biblical times were called fullers. They would wash clothes by stamping them or beating them with a stick in a tub of water. It was such a smelly business that it had to be done outside the city walls! (2 Kings 18:17, Isaiah 7:3, Mark 9:3, KJV)

Who was named after David?

No one! Even though David was one of the great heroes in the Bible, no one was ever named after him. He is the only David in the Bible.

THE ONE AND ONLY DAVID

13

In his first letter, Peter calls somebody the "Head Shepherd." Who is it?
Peter is talking about Jesus, who watches over the flock of God.
(1 Peter 5:1-4, TLB)

What woman was both a leader in Israel and a prophet?
Deborah was the woman who brought the Israelites back to God after they had sinned against the Lord. And, with the help of Barak, Deborah also defeated King Jabin's army, which included 900 chariots.
(Judges 4–5)

What kind of towel did Mary use to wipe Jesus' feet after she poured perfume on them?
She didn't—she used her hair! (John 12:1-3)

The answer to this is probably on the tip of your tongue. What did God do to Isaiah to forgive and purify him?

In a vision in the temple, an angel picked out a burning coal from the altar with a pair of tongs. Then he touched the prophet's mouth with it. (Isaiah 6:6-7)

One person woke up in his prison cell and—that very night—went to bed in a palace. Who was he?
Joseph was a slave in Egypt, but when he was able to interpret the pharaoh's dream, he was made a ruler of the country. (Genesis 41)

The prophet Elisha was walking along the road from Jericho to Bethel when he met a gang of young men. They started making fun of him. Why?
They teased him because he was bald. Elisha cursed them and two bears came out of the woods and attacked them. (2 Kings 2:23-24)

Who was known as a crazy driver?

King Jehu had a reputation for driving his chariot very fast. Watchmen could sometimes spot him from far away because of the way he drove! (2 Kings 9:16-20, TLB)

Who liked having a crowd with him wherever he went?

Absalom hired 50 men to run ahead of him every time he went out in his chariot. (2 Samuel 15:1)

Who had a truly hair-raising experience?

Eliphaz. One night in a vision, a spirit glided past his face. Eliphaz was so scared that the hair on his body stood on end! (Job 4:12-15)

KIDS LONG AGO

How old was Joash when he became king of Judah?
Joash was seven years old. His Aunt Jehosheba had hidden him from his grandmother, who wished him dead, for six years. (2 Kings 11:1-3, 21; 2 Chronicles 22:11-12)

What judge in Israel had 70 sons?
Gideon. (Judges 8:30)

Two women both claimed to be the mother of one baby. How did King Solomon decide who was telling the truth?
Instead of asking lots of questions, Solomon ordered them to cut the baby in half. He guessed that the real mother would give up the baby to save its life—and he was right. (1 Kings 3:16-28)

Who was only eight when he became king of Judah?
Josiah. He was especially obedient to God's law and became known for destroying idol worship. (2 Kings 22:1–23:30)

Where did Moses' mother hide him so that he wouldn't be killed by the Egyptian pharaoh?
She hid him at home for three months, then she made a little boat out of papyrus reeds and hid it at the edge of the Nile River. As it turns out, the pharaoh's daughter rescued him. (Exodus 2:1-10)

How did Jesus help Jairus, the leader of a synagogue?
Jairus's daughter was very ill and died before Jesus could get to her house. But Jesus brought her back to life! (Mark 5:22-23, 35-43; Luke 8:41-56)

What happened to a 17-year-old when he told his family about a dream?
Joseph, who was his father's favourite son, told his brothers that in his dream their bundles of grain bowed down before his. They got so angry they sold him into slavery! (Genesis 37:1-28)

But it was only a dream!

What young boy taught at the Temple in Jerusalem?
Jesus, who was only 12 years old at the time, taught the teachers of the Law. The teachers were very clever men, but they were amazed by Jesus' knowledge. (Luke 2:41-47)

What was rubbed all over a newborn baby in biblical times?
After the baby was washed clean, salt was rubbed over the body. This was probably done because the salt acted as a disinfectant. (Ezekiel 16:4)

What orphan girl became a queen of Medo-Persia?

Esther, who was not only an orphan but a Hebrew slave as well, became queen when King Ahasuerus married her. The Old Testament book with her name tells her story.

Who became a king of Judah at the age of 12 and did just about everything wrong?

Manasseh. The son of Hezekiah, he ruled for 55 years but led the people in the wrong kind of worship, built hilltop shrines to idols, and got into black magic. (2 Kings 21:1-18)

What did God have to do to get a message through to Samuel?

God called Samuel three times while the boy slept, but each time Samuel thought it was the voice of Eli, the priest whom he served. Eli told him to say, "Yes, Lord, I'm listening!" if it happened again. It did, and the Lord was with Samuel from then on. (1 Samuel 3:1-19)

SAMUEL, I HAVE A MESSAGE

21

What was Daniel's three-year diet plan?

Daniel, Hananiah, Mishael, and Azariah were among the boys in a three-year training programme to serve King Nebuchadnezzar of Babylon. The four boys decided that instead of eating the best foods and wine the king offered, they would keep themselves pure and eat only vegetables and water. At the end of three years, Daniel and his friends turned out to be the healthiest and wisest of the group. (Daniel 1)

Who had brothers named James, Joseph, Simon, and Judas?

Jesus! (Matthew 13:55, Mark 6:3)

Why did the strongest man in the world need a little boy's help?

Samson had been captured, blinded, and put in prison by the Philistines. They wanted to make fun of him, so he was brought to the centre of their temple. Samson asked a little boy to place his hands on the temple pillars. With God's help, Samson pushed the pillars down and the temple collapsed. Samson and over 3,000 people died—more than he had killed in his lifetime. (Judges 16:23-30, TLB)

22

Who taught Timothy about God when he was growing up?
His mother, Eunice, and his grandmother Lois taught him. And they taught him well because Timothy grew up to become a missionary and Paul's helper.
(2 Timothy 1:5)

Which teenager really "dug dirt"?
Uzziah. He became king of Judah when he was 16 years old and was known for his love of the soil because he had so many farms and vineyards. (2 Chronicles 26:1, 10)

Jephthah's promise to God cost him something very special. What was it?
His only daughter. Because God had helped Jephthah defeat the Ammonites, Jephthah promised to make a sacrifice of whatever came out of his house to meet him when he returned home from battle. Jephthah's only daughter ran out to greet her father when he returned. (Judges 11:30-35)

23

Which priest spoiled his sons?

Eli. His sons were so spoiled that they didn't respect God, and because of that, God promised that their sins would never be forgiven by sacrifices or offerings. (1 Samuel 3:13-14)

Moses and Aaron were brothers who grew up to be important leaders of Israel. Who was older?

Aaron—by three years. (Exodus 7:7)

Whose children caused so much trouble that their family had to move?

Jacob's. King Hamor's son, Shechem, had fallen in love with Jacob's daughter, Dinah, and wanted to marry her. But Dinah's brothers, Simeon and Levi, didn't approve of Shechem, so they went to the city where he lived and killed all the men. Jacob was so upset by what happened that he moved his family to the town of Bethel. (Genesis 34, 35:1)

24

Which king probably had to listen to a lot of girl talk?
Rehoboam. He had 60 daughters!
(2 Chronicles 11:21)

Who was one of the best-dressed children in the Bible?
Joseph. Joseph's father, Jacob, who was a shepherd, gave Joseph a brightly-coloured coat. It was like the coats that royalty often wore.
(Genesis 37:3)

Who was born with an ID bracelet?
Zerah. When Tamar was giving birth to her twin sons, the midwife tied a red thread around the wrist of the child who appeared first. But he pulled back his hand and the other baby was actually born first. After that, the baby with the red thread on his wrist was born. He was named Zerah. (Genesis 38:27-30)

Which disciple was probably a twin?
Thomas, whose nickname was "the twin." (John 11:16)

What did it mean when Naomi took her daughter-in-law's son, Obed, onto her lap after he was born?
It symbolized that Naomi wanted to adopt Obed and treat him as her own child. With this action, Naomi gained an heir in place of her sons who had died. (Ruth 4:14-17)

What surprising image does the prophet Isaiah use to describe a time of peace?
A little child. He says that there will be peace when a little child leads the wild beasts. (Isaiah 11:6)

WHAT'S IN A WORD... OR A NUMBER?

Who was the oldest man in the Bible?
Methuselah, who was Noah's grandfather, lived to be 969! (Genesis 5:25-27)

What's the most popular name in the Bible?
Twenty-seven men had the name Shemaiah.

What was the nickname for missionaries who had other jobs?
Missionaries who knew other trades were sometimes called "tentmakers" because the apostle Paul, known for his preaching and teaching, sometimes made tents to earn money. This nickname is still used today. (Acts 18:1-3)

Who gave their son a name meaning "laughter"?
Sarah and Abraham named their son Isaac, which means "laughter," because they were happy to finally have a son in their old age. (Genesis 17:19, 21:3)

How many wives did King Solomon have?
Solomon, who ruled for 40 years, had 700 wives! (1 Kings 11:3)

Which of Jesus' disciples was nicknamed "Rock"?
The apostle Peter's original name was Simon. Jesus named him Petros, or Peter, which means "rock" in Greek. Jesus declared that Peter's faith would be the foundation rock on which the church would be built. (Matthew 16:17-18)

Why is Exodus the perfect name for the second book of the Old Testament?
The word *exodus* means a departure of a large number of people, and the book Exodus tells how the Israelites—about 600,000 men, with their wives, children, animals, and belongings—fled Egypt and set out on foot into the desert. (Exodus 12:31-38)

When the Israelites made their journey out of Egypt, they ate something called "What is it?" when translated. What was it?
They ate *manna* in the desert, which were probably thin white wafers that tasted like honey. (Exodus 16:31)

What would you be doing if you used a homer, an ephah, and a bath?
Measuring liquids or dry goods. Ten ephahs equalled one homer of dry goods, and ten baths equalled one homer of liquid. A homer was about five bushels. (Ezekiel 45:11)

How many people did Jesus feed for lunch one day?
A group of 5,000 had gathered to listen to Jesus, and with one boy's lunch of five loaves and two fishes, Jesus fed the whole crowd. And 12 baskets were filled with leftovers! (John 6:1-13)

What elderly couple had their names changed by God when he promised they finally were to become parents?
Sarai became Sarah ("princess") and Abram became Abraham ("father of nations"). (Genesis 17:1-19)

In John's Revelation, how were the 144,000 people chosen by God marked?
The people from each of the 12 tribes of Israel had the Seal of God put on their foreheads. (Revelation 7:3-8)

What's the longest name in the Bible?
That honor belongs to Maher-shalal-hash-baz, son of the prophet Isaiah. God told Isaiah to give his son that name, which means "your enemies will soon be destroyed." (Isaiah 8:1)

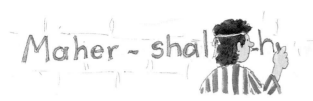

Jacob had his name changed by God later in his life. What was his new name and what did it mean?
God changed Jacob's name to Israel, which means "one who struggles with God" because he had wrestled with an angel. (Genesis 32:22-30, 35:9-10)

Where do we get the saying "I can see the writing on the wall"?
King Belshazzar invited more than 1,000 people to a great feast. Suddenly a giant hand started writing on the wall! Only Daniel could tell what the words meant—judgment and destruction. (Daniel 5)

32

The Gospel of Matthew says that when Jesus was on the cross, it was dark "from the sixth hour to the ninth hour." What time does this mean on our clocks?
From 12 noon to 3 p.m.
(Matthew 27:45)

Just how big was Goliath?
The Philistine giant that David fought was over 270 cm tall! He wore a bronze helmet, a 90 kg coat of mail, and bronze leggings. His bronze spear was so huge that it was several centimetres thick in diameter and was tipped with a 11 kg iron spearhead.
(1 Samuel 17:4-7)

Whose name means "grabber"?
Jacob was given that name because he was holding on to his twin brother Esau's heel when they were born.
(Genesis 25:24-26)

Whose name—which is also the name of a book in the Bible—means "messenger"?
Malachi.

Whose name was "for the birds"?
Jonah. His name means "dove."

What does the word Bible *mean?*
The word *Bible* comes from the Latin and the Greek word *biblia*, which means "the books." The earliest use of *biblia* for what we call the Bible is believed to be about 150 A.D. Daniel learned from the early prophecies, which he called "the books." The New Testament talks about parts of the Old Testament and uses such words as "the Scriptures" or "the sacred writings." (Daniel 9:2, Matthew 21:42, 2 Timothy 3:15-16, 2 Peter 3:16)

34

Who changed her own name from a word meaning "pleasant," to a word meaning "bitter"?
Ruth's mother-in-law, Naomi (meaning "pleasant"), was so upset when her husband and sons died that from then on she wanted to be called Mara (meaning "bitter"). (Ruth 1:20)

Which queen had a "heavenly" name?
Esther. Her name means "star."

Which loving, unselfish woman in the Bible was "something worth seeing"?
Ruth. Her name means exactly that—"something worth seeing."

Which prophet had a very "heavy" name?
Amos. His name means "one with a burden."

Which apostle had a very "bright" name?
Luke. His name means "light-giving."

Which troubled man had a name that suited him perfectly?
Job. His name means "he that weeps," and he lost everything he owned.

THE LIVING WORLD

In the Bible, the ostrich is famous for two qualities. What are they?
The ostrich was considered stupid because it laid its eggs on the sand, not caring that someone might crush them. It was also able to run faster than a horse. (An adult ostrich can run at speeds of almost 80 miles per hour.) (Job 39:13-18)

Which animal is called the "behemoth," or water monster, in the book of Job?
When God speaks to Job about the strength of this animal, he is talking about the hippopotamus, according to Bible scholars. It no longer lives in Bible lands but did until about the 12th century. (Job 40:15)

Solomon brought horses to Israel from Egypt and other countries. What were they used for?
Horses, which were symbols of power, were usually reserved for war. Solomon himself had 40,000 chariot horses. Ordinary travelling was done on donkeys. (1 Kings 4:26)

What two animals would you never see ploughing together on an Israelite's farm?
An ox and a donkey. The Israelites believed that things that are not alike should not be mixed, including animals. (Deuteronomy 22:10)

Israelites weren't allowed to keep a certain animal that we see on many farms today. What was it?
They weren't allowed to keep pigs because they were the symbol of everything bad and were forbidden as food. (Leviticus 11:7, Deuteronomy 14:8)

So long!

How was the prophet Jonah saved after being thrown overboard from a ship?
God sent a "great fish," which was probably a whale, to swallow him and keep him safe for three days and three nights. Several kinds of toothed whales lived in the sea where Jonah sailed, and some were large enough to swallow a human being. In the 20th century this has actually happened, and some people have lived to tell the tale! (Jonah 1:17)

Today we know that the bat is a mammal. What did the early Hebrews think it was?
They considered the bat a bird. It was listed among the unclean birds that the people of Israel could not eat. (Leviticus 11:13-19)

Sheep...that's 7 pairs...check!

How many pairs of each animal did Noah take into the ark?
Noah took seven pairs of every kind of bird and seven pairs of every kind of "clean" animal. But he only took one pair of every kind of "unclean" animal, meaning those that couldn't be eaten. (Genesis 7:1-4)

What animal did people use as an alarm clock in biblical times?
The cock, because it woke up early and started crowing. Even today people depend on it. (Mark 13:35)

COCK-A-DOODLE-DO!

What famous U.S. symbol did the early Hebrews believe was immortal?
The eagle. They believed it could renew its youth as it aged so that it would always be swift and strong. (Psalm 103:5)

How were some birds used like calendars?
The Hebrews knew that some birds were very regular in their migration times, especially the large, slow-flying storks that migrated along the Jordan River Valley in spring. (Jeremiah 8:7)

How did we get the expression "a little bird told me"?
The book of Ecclesiastes warns people that if they say bad things about the king, the birds will act as telltales. (Ecclesiastes 10:20)

When Job lost his fortune and his family, what did he say had become his friend?
He complained that he had become "a companion of owls." Owls were often the symbols of sadness and loneliness. (Job 30:29)

Not to pull the wool over your eyes, but what animal is mentioned the most in the Bible?
Flocks of sheep roamed the hills and valleys of the Holy Land. They are mentioned 742 times in the Bible.

What was as frightening as an invading army?
Locusts, which are like grasshoppers, often moved in swarms of thousands. These swarms could wipe out all the crops in a country and cause a famine. (Isaiah 33:4)

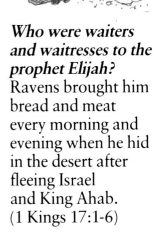

What part of the wild ox did the Israelites sometimes use to carry water?
The ox had horns so big that they could hold up to 18 litres of water.

What strange vision did Peter have before he met Cornelius? What did it mean?
Peter saw a big sheet full of "unclean" animals, snakes, and birds, and a voice told him to eat them. God used the vision to show Peter how he should accept all kinds of people. (Acts 10)

Who were waiters and waitresses to the prophet Elijah?
Ravens brought him bread and meat every morning and evening when he hid in the desert after fleeing Israel and King Ahab. (1 Kings 17:1-6)

Before all his troubles, Job had an amazing number of livestock: 7,000 sheep, 3,000 camels, 500 teams of oxen, and 500 female donkeys. What did he have at the end of his life? The Lord rewarded Job for his faith by giving him back twice as many animals as he had had before. (Job 1:1-3, 42:12)

When the Bible mentions "the song of the turtle" in the Song of Solomon 2:12, does it really mean "reptile music"? No. "Turtle" in this case means "turtledove," a common bird in biblical times. Pairs of turtledoves were often offered as sacrifices, as Joseph and Mary did when Jesus was a baby. (Luke 2:24)

The Israelites were not permitted to eat pigs. Were they allowed to eat insects? Yes! The Bible specifies that insects that fly and walk or crawl could not be eaten, but insects that jump, such as grasshoppers, locusts, and crickets, could be considered food. (Leviticus 11:20-23)

Where were the Israelites able to get water when they were out in the wild?

From a rock! When the Israelites were wandering through the wilderness, they camped at a place where there wasn't any water. Moses prayed to God to help him, and God told Moses to take his walking stick and strike a rock. He did and water gushed out of it. (Exodus 17:1-7)

Ooooh! Nice chains!

Who were the best-dressed animals in the Bible?

Probably the camels belonging to the Midianites. These camels, used for desert travel, actually wore gold chains around their necks. (Judges 8:26)

Which wild animal appears most often in the Bible?

The lion is mentioned about 130 times and was widely seen in Old Testament times. Just as today, it was a symbol of strength and of royalty. It was also an important part of an exciting story about Daniel! (Daniel 6)

WOE! WOE!

What did Solomon ride to the place where he was to be crowned king?
Solomon rode a mule that belonged to his father, David. When Jesus rode into Jerusalem on a donkey, he showed that he too was a king. (1 Kings 1:32-35, Matthew 21:1-7)

What's the only talking bird in the Bible?
An eagle! It flies about crying, "Woe! Woe!" (Revelation 8:13)

How did a goat take away the sins of the Israelites?
God told Aaron to take a goat into the Tabernacle, lay his hands on its head, and confess all the sins of Israel over it. The goat was then led into the wilderness, taking the sins with it. (Leviticus 16: 20-22)

THE NATURAL WORLD

What kinds of "fruits" can be produced in us?
In his letter to the Galatians, Paul says that with the Holy Spirit in our lives, the "fruits" of love, patience, joy, peace, kindness, goodness, and faith will grow in us. (Galatians 5:22-23)

Why did the prophet Elijah have one of the worst days in the Bible?
He experienced a powerful wind, an earthquake, and a supernatural fire all in one day! (1 Kings 19:11-13)

Why is Mount Sinai sacred?
It was the mountain where Moses received the Ten Commandments from God. Mount Sinai was thought to be so sacred that any person— or even animal—that touched the mountain had to be killed by stoning or by arrows. (Exodus 19:20-23)

A picture of what fruit was embroidered on the high priest's robe?

The pomegranate was considered so special that blue, purple, and red images of the fruit were put on the edge of the robe. The pomegranate was special because its fruit could be eaten, its juice was drinkable, and its blooms could be made into medicine. (Exodus 28:33-34)

What was poured on Saul's and David's heads when they were made kings of Israel?

The prophet Samuel used olive oil to anoint them. (1 Samuel 10:1, 16:13)

What kind of tree did King Solomon use when building his famous temple?

Solomon used the cedar of Lebanon, the largest tree in biblical lands. It towered as high as 40 metres and the diameter of its trunk could reach 240 cm. (1 Kings 5:6)

What caused Absalom's doom?
When Absalom was running away on his mule from David's men, he rode under a tree and his long hair got caught in the branches. David's men found him and killed him. (2 Samuel 18:9-15)

What did Elijah use to start a fire?
Water! Elijah had barrels of water poured on the altar the Israelites were using, and suddenly God set it ablaze. (1 Kings 18:30-38)

What happened when Aaron hit the surface of the Nile River with his rod?
The river turned to blood. But the pharaoh's magicians were able to do the same thing, so the pharaoh wasn't impressed. (Exodus 7:15-24)

What weather forecast did the prophet Elijah give to King Ahab?

Ahab was a wicked king and didn't worship the Lord. Because of this, Elijah told Ahab that there wouldn't be dew or rain for three years. Elijah's prediction came true, and drought and famine covered the land. (1 Kings 16:29 – 18:2)

In the Revelation to John, what did he see fall from Heaven?

John saw hailstones weighing 45 kg falling from the sky. Look out below! (Revelation 16:21)

What did Moses use as a water sweetener?

A tree. The Israelites had been walking through the desert for three days without water. They came to Marah, but couldn't drink the water there because it was bitter. God showed Moses a tree and told him to throw it in the water. When Moses did this, the water became sweet. (Exodus 15:22-26)

What did Peter catch once while he was fishing?
He caught a fish with a coin in its mouth! Jesus told Peter to use the coin to pay the taxes for both of them. (Matthew 17:24-27)

Manna again!

The Israelites didn't miss being slaves once they left Egypt, but what did they miss?
The food! The Israelites complained to Moses that they missed things like fish, cucumbers, melons, onions, and garlic. (Numbers 11:4-5)

Who had such a terrible fight that the earth moved?
Korah and some of the other Israelites argued with Moses and Aaron because they didn't want them to be their leaders anymore. God was so angry at Korah and the other men that he made the ground split open and swallow them up! (Numbers 16:1-35)

Why did Jesus get upset over some spices?
The teachers of the Law and the Pharisees were very careful about tithing—giving a tenth of everything that they had to God. But Jesus said that they should pay less attention to weighing out mint, dill, and cumin and more attention to showing justice, mercy, and faithfulness. (Matthew 23:23)

Who listened to a bush?
Moses. God appeared to him as a bush that was on fire but didn't burn up. God told Moses he had chosen him to lead the Israelites out of Egypt. (Exodus 3:1-10)

What unusual road map did the Israelites use once they fled Egypt?
God guided the Israelites through the desert with a pillar of cloud during the day and a pillar of fire at night. (Exodus 13:17-22)

What nutty gift did Jacob send to Joseph in Egypt?
Pistachio nuts and almonds were among the things Jacob and Joseph's brothers sent as gifts. (Genesis 43:11)

Who saw a sea of glass?
John. (Revelation 4:6)

What "household" tree did Elijah sit under?
He rested under a broom tree. The broom tree was actually a desert shrub, often large enough for someone to sit under. (1 Kings 19:4)

Jacob probably didn't have a good night's sleep as he travelled to Haran. Why not?
He used a stone for a pillow! (Genesis 28:10-11)

What very sticky river did Zophar speak about?
A river of honey. (Job 20:17)

Shhh! Here she comes!

Where was the secret hiding place of Obadiah and 100 prophets?
Two caves. Obadiah hid 50 prophets in each cave from Queen Jezebel, who was trying to kill them. (1 Kings 18:3-4)

What did Jonah use as a sun shelter in the desert?
A vine. God made a vine spring up miraculously over Jonah to give him shade from the hot sun. (Jonah 4:6)

Solomon compared good advice to what expensive fruit?
Gold apples—in a silver basket! (Proverbs 25:11)

What large plant, according to the New Testament, has tiny beginnings?
The mustard plant. Jesus said that the Kingdom of Heaven is like a mustard plant; although it starts as the smallest of all seeds, it grows into a tree where birds can build nests. (Matthew 13:31-32)

CITIES, CIVILIZATIONS & STRUCTURES

What town is believed to be the oldest in the world?
Jericho, which Joshua and the Israelites attacked when they entered Canaan. It had double walls 9 metres high, and each was 2 metres thick. Five ancient cities have been built on that spot. (Joshua 6)

You'll like it here. It's a nice old city...

Who rebuilt the city of Jericho, and what awful price did he pay for completing the task?
When King Ahab ruled Israel, Hiel of Bethel rebuilt Jericho. When Hiel laid the foundations, his firstborn son, Abiram, died. When he set up the gates, his son Segub died. This was God's curse on Jericho which Joshua had predicted. (1 Kings 16:34)

What were 8 metres high and 5 metres around?
The two pillars for Solomon's Temple—they were huge and made of hollow bronze. Their walls were 10 cm thick. The decorations at the top of each pillar, also made of bronze, were 220 cm tall. (1 Kings 7:15-22, TLB)

Who did Solomon "hire" to guard the inner room of his temple?
The inner room was the place where the Ark of the Covenant was kept. Solomon put two statues of guardian angels there. They were each 4 metres high and were made of olive wood covered with gold. Their outer wings reached from wall to wall. (1 Kings 6:23-28)

King Hezekiah of Judah was known for his wise and God-fearing ways. What did he do for Jerusalem?
He made a pool and a channel and brought water into the city. (2 Kings 20:20)

This is our daughter.

When is a daughter not the female child of a man or woman?
Some of the larger towns in biblical times controlled villages in the countryside. These villages were called "daughters," though they are often referred to as "surrounding settlements" in the Bible today. They probably helped supply the main town with food. (2 Chronicles 28:18, Nehemiah 11:25-31)

What giant-sized wedding gift did the Egyptian pharaoh give when King Solomon married his daughter?

The pharaoh gave the couple the entire city of Gezer. (1 Kings 9:16)

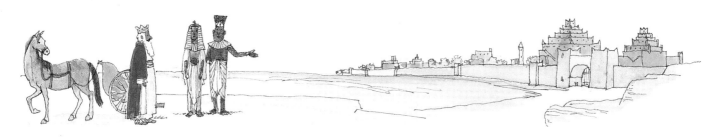

Moses sent 12 spies into Canaan when the Israelite first arrived there after leaving Egypt. What was their report?

They were impressed with the good fruit that grew there, but they said that the native people were tall and frightening. When the Israelites heard this, the grew afraid and refused to take the land as God commanded them to do. So God punished them b making them wander in the wilderness for many more years.
(Numbers 13–14)

How many years did it take to build Solomon's palace?

It was so grand that it took 13 years! One of the rooms was 45 metres long, 23 metres wide, and 13 metres high. It had 45 windows!
(1 Kings 7:1-4, TLB)

How did Heaven get the nickname of "the pearly gates"?
John's Revelation describes 12 city gates—each made from a single pearl—in the New Jerusalem, or Heaven. (Revelation 21:21)

What was the royal colour in biblical times?
Purple was the colour of kings and queens then…and now. The purple dye used in ancient times came from a snail. Thousands of snails were needed for a tiny amount of dye, so only the rich could afford to buy purple garments. (Exodus 25:4, Judges 8:26)

What is the first building mentioned in the Bible, and what was it built to do?
The Tower of Babel was meant to be a kind of stairway to Heaven. But God put a stop to its construction by giving the builders different languages so they couldn't understand each other. (Genesis 11:1-9)

61

Why did God forbid David to build the Temple?
After David had gathered all the material to build the Temple of the Lord, God told him he could not because he had killed too many men in battle. David's son, Solomon, a man of peace, built the Temple. (1 Chronicles 22:2-10)

What city was nicknamed "city of palm trees"?
Jericho. The name Jericho itself probably means "moon city."

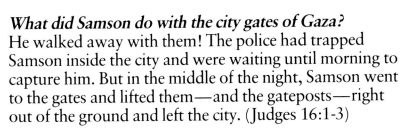

What did Samson do with the city gates of Gaza?
He walked away with them! The police had trapped Samson inside the city and were waiting until morning to capture him. But in the middle of the night, Samson went to the gates and lifted them—and the gateposts—right out of the ground and left the city. (Judges 16:1-3)

You probably could have heard people whistling while they worked on the Temple of the Lord. Why?
The stones used to build the Temple were already cut and smoothed at the quarry, so the Temple was built without the sound of hammers, chisels, and axes. (1 Kings 6:7)

Where would you find the Fish Gate, the Sheep Gate, and the Tower of the Ovens?
These were all part of the wall around the city of Jerusalem. Nehemiah tells how they were rebuilt after being destroyed by Israel's enemies. (Nehemiah 3)

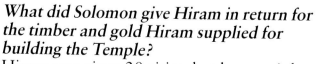

What did Solomon give Hiram in return for the timber and gold Hiram supplied for building the Temple?
Hiram was given 20 cities, but he wasn't happy with the payment! (1 Kings 9:10-12)

What did Paul say in his "pep talk" to the Corinthians?
The city of Corinth was famous for its athletic games. So in his letter to the Corinthians, Paul compared the Christian life to a footrace, a time of training for a fight, and other sports. (1 Corinthians 9:24-27)

What city in Canaan was "destroyed" by the Israelites?
Ai, which means "ruin."
(Joshua 8:3-29)

What's a parapet and why did every Hebrew house have to have one?
A parapet was a kind of guardrail for the roof, where people often spent time. One of the laws required a parapet so that a home-owner wouldn't be to blame if someone fell from the roof. (Deuteronomy 22:8)

To what city did Paul send his longest letter?
Rome. (His letter to the Romans.)

What city was "Satan's seat" according to John?
Pergamos. John called it this because the city was the official centre of emperor worship in Asia. (Revelation 2:12-13)

From here to here....

Dan

The Great Sea

Sea of Galilee

Jerusalem

Dead Sea

Beersheba

What two cities were often considered the northern and southern limits of Israel?
Dan, in the north, and Beersheba, in the south. (Judges 20:1, 2 Chronicles 30:5)

What biblical city was often just referred to as Zion?
Jerusalem.

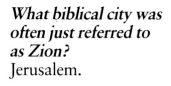

In what city will there be no need for lamps?
The New Jerusalem—or Heaven—because the glory of God will give it light. (Revelation 22:5)

What city had lukewarm citizens?
Laodicea. In his letter to the leader of the church in that city, John said that the people of Laodicea were neither hot nor cold. He was telling the citizens that they needed to be committed to their faith in God. (Revelation 3:14-16)

STRANGER THAN EVER!

What was Saul doing when the prophet Samuel came to make him the first king of Israel?
Saul was out hunting some lost donkeys that belonged to his father. (1 Samuel 9:1-20)

Jeremiah says that an idol is like something you might see in a garden. What is it?
Jeremiah says that idols are like scarecrows because they cannot speak and cannot walk. (Jeremiah 10:5)

When Peter was in prison, an angel helped him escape. What did the two Roman guards do?
They slept through the whole thing! (Acts 12:1-9)

How much food did it take to feed Solomon's household?
Among other things, they used 195 bushels of flour, and prepared 30 cows and 100 sheep every day.
(1 Kings 4:20-23, TLB)

Dinnertime!

In ancient times, why was it a pain in the neck to lose?
After a battle, the winner often stepped on the neck of someone he had beaten as a symbol of his victory.
(Lamentations 5:5, TLB)

Which prophet was told by God to eat a book?
God told Ezekiel to eat a book and then go and give its message to the people of Israel. When Ezekiel ate the book, it tasted like honey!
(Ezekiel 3:1-4)

What happened to Zechariah when the angel Gabriel told him that he and his wife Elizabeth would have a son?
Because Zechariah didn't believe Gabriel, the angel told him he wouldn't be able to speak until the child was born. (Luke 1)

In ancient Israel, there was a custom that if you were giving up your right to buy something, you had to give up something else, too. What was it?
Your sandal. (Ruth 4:7)

Many people can tell others what their dreams mean. But Daniel did something much better—what was it?
Daniel told King Nebuchadnezzar what he had dreamed as well as what it meant. (Daniel 2)

What did Agabus do to show what would happen to Paul in Jerusalem?
Agabus took Paul's belt and tied up his own hands and feet. He said that the Jews would tie up Paul this way and turn him over to the Romans.
(Acts 21:10-11)

In his letter, Jude talks about an argument between the angel Michael and Satan. About what did they argue?
Moses' body. (Jude 1:9)

Who woke up in the morning after his wedding and discovered he had married the wrong woman?
Jacob. He had agreed to work for his Uncle Laban for seven years so that he could marry Rachel. But on the morning after the wedding, he discovered that his uncle had tricked him, and that he had married Leah, Rachel's older sister, instead. He had to work another seven years to marry the woman he wanted to marry!
(Genesis 29:16-30)

What was unusual about the prophet Balaam's donkey?

She talked! The donkey spoke to Balaam because he had hit her when she refused to keep walking. But the donkey had only been trying to warn Balaam about an angel that stood in the road. (Numbers 22:22-31)

Who left his friends speechless?

Job. He had suffered a lot, and his three best friends decided to visit him. When they saw how much pain Job was in, they were so sad they couldn't say a word, and sat in silence with Job for seven days and nights. (Job 2:11-13)

How many men were in the largest army?

General Zerah of Ethiopia led an army of one million men! But they were defeated by King Asa of Judah, who had an army of only 580,000 men. (2 Chronicles 14:8-12)

The gifts the wise men gave the baby Jesus predicted the future. How?
All three gifts were prophetic and not typical baby gifts, even in those times. The gold spoke of Jesus' coming kingship. Frankincense, used in sacrificial services, pointed to his being a priest. Perhaps the strangest gift for a baby was myrrh—a spice used in many anointing ceremonies and used to prepare Jesus' body for burial. (Matthew 2:11, John 19:39-40)

YUCK!! HALF BAKED!

Why did the Israelites belong in a bakery?
God once said that the Israelites were as useless as a half-baked cake because they were worshipping other people's gods. (Hosea 7:8)

Why should Lot's wife have kept her eyes on the road?
The people of Sodom and Gomorrah had turned against God, so he decided to destroy the cities. God warned Lot of his plan and told him to take his family and escape, but that they must not look back as they fled. As they were leaving, Lot's wife looked back and was turned into a pillar of salt! (Genesis 19:17-26)

Who was called "a living rock"?
Jesus. Peter said that Christ is the living rock upon which God builds. (1 Peter 2:4)

What nation did God toss his sandal on?
Edom. This might refer to the act by which someone claimed a right to something. (Psalm 60:8)

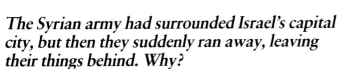

The Syrian army had surrounded Israel's capital city, but then they suddenly ran away, leaving their things behind. Why?
During the night, God made the sound of a huge army of speeding chariots and galloping horses. The Syrians thought the Israelites had joined forces with two other armies, and they fled in fear. (2 Kings 7:6-7)

Martha and Mary were very sad when Jesus came to visit them, but they were overjoyed by the time he left. Why?
When Jesus came to visit Martha and Mary they told him that their brother Lazarus had died four days before. Jesus went to the tomb and raised Lazarus to life again! (John 11:17-44)

What city did God put sandals on?
Jerusalem. This is a reference to how God looked after Jerusalem. (Ezekiel 16:10)

What kind of strange food were snakes believed to eat?
The people of Israel believed that snakes ate dust! (Genesis 3:14, Isaiah 65:25)

Jesus said a poor widow could give away more money than a rich man. How?
Because she had so little, what she gave was a much greater sacrifice than what the rich man gave. (Luke 21:1-4)

What did Jesus use to heal a deaf man and then a blind man?
His own spit! (Mark 7:31-37, 8:22-25)

What made Egypt so "jumpy" about the power of God?
God sent a plague of frogs that covered every corner of the land to show them his power. (Exodus 8:1-6)

DID YOU KNOW?

What kind of food do you serve to an angel?
When Gideon, a judge of Israel, was visited by an angel, he served him roasted goat, bread, and broth. (Judges 6:19)

What famous U.S. landmark is engraved with Leviticus 25:10 on its side, "Proclaim liberty throughout the land to all its inhabitants"?
The Liberty Bell in Philadelphia, Pennsylvania.

Many prophets started their "careers" as priests and were well educated. But what was Amos's job before God called him to speak?
He was a shepherd and a fruit picker. (Amos 1:1, 7:14-15)

Why did Paul decide to go to Macedonia (part of Greece) to preach?

In a vision, Paul saw a man in Macedonia begging him, "Come over here and help us!" Sometimes God's message can't get any clearer! (Acts 16:9-10)

What did the four friends of a paralyzed man do to get through the crowds around Jesus?

They dug a hole in a clay roof and let him down on a stretcher! Jesus forgave the man's sins and healed him. (Mark 2:1-12)

When Paul was in prison, what did he ask Timothy to bring him?

The only things Paul wanted were his coat, some books (scrolls), and some parchments (the material they used for paper in those days). (2 Timothy 4:9-13)

To what does the prophet Jeremiah compare the kingdom of Babylon?
Jeremiah calls Babylon the biggest hammer in all the earth, but says one day it will lie broken. (Jeremiah 50:22-25)

YOU 20 OR OLDER?

Who started the first army draft?
Eleazar, Aaron's son, recruited all the Israelite men who were 20 years old or older to serve as soldiers. (Numbers 26:1-2)

What happened to Eutychus when he listened to one of Paul's very long sermons?
Eutychus fell asleep while sitting in an open window, fell out the window to the ground three storeys below, and died! Paul went downstairs, picked him up, and brought Eutychus back to life. (Acts 20:7-12, TLB)

Who never needs any sleep?
God doesn't need to sleep. He is always watching over all people, and he never slumbers or sleeps. (Psalm 121:3-4)

What jewellery did the tribe of Ishmael like to wear?
They all wore gold earrings. (Judges 8:24)

Who cooked his friends a very special breakfast?
Jesus. One day, some of the disciples were fishing, and when they came to shore they saw a fire with some fish cooking over it. To their surprise, there was Jesus—who had been crucified and had risen from the dead—making breakfast for them! (John 21:7-12)

How much did the prophet Hosea have to pay to buy his wife back from slavery?
Hosea gave just a little money and eight bushels of barley to get his wife, Gomer, back. (Hosea 3:2, TLB)

Shamgar, one of the judges of Israel, once killed 600 Philistines. What amazing weapon did he use?
Shamgar used an ox goad, which is simply a long-handled stick used to move animals along. (Judges 3:31)

Once David's troops fought a tribe of giants at Gath. What was extra special about one of the giants?
He had 12 fingers and 12 toes! (2 Samuel 21:20-21)

Aaron's staff was very special. Why?
When Pharaoh asked Moses and Aaron to perform a miracle, Aaron turned his staff into a snake! Pharaoh's magicians were able to perform the same feat, but Aaron's snake ate the magicians' snakes! (Exodus 7:8-12)

What important instructions did an angel give Samson's mother before Samson was born?
The angel told her not to eat grapes or raisins or anything that the Israelites weren't allowed to eat, not to drink any wine or beer, and most importantly—not to cut Samson's hair! (Judges 13:1-5)

Who gave Samson his only haircut?
A barber. Although Delilah got Samson to tell her the secret of his strength, she herself did not cut his hair. When he fell asleep, Delilah called the Philistine leaders, and they sent for a barber. (Judges 16:4-22)

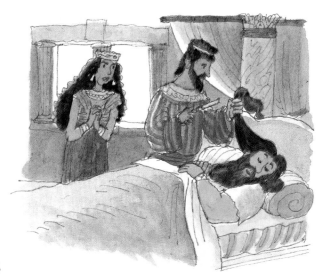

What prophet saw a very strong bird?
Ezekiel. He saw a large eagle with multi-coloured feathers that carried off the top of a cedar tree. (Ezekiel 17:3-4)

Most brothers swop football cards or toys. What swop did Esau and Jacob make?
Esau came home from hunting one day and was so hungry that he swopped his right to be the head of the family for a bowl of the stew Jacob was cooking! (Genesis 25:29-34)

Whom did Jesus save from a sinking experience?
Peter. One night the apostles were on a boat during a storm. Jesus walked out to them across the water. Peter tried to walk across the water to Jesus, but got scared and began to sink. Jesus reached out and saved him. (Matthew 14:22-33)

How many years were the Israelites in Egypt?
430! (Exodus 12:40)

Who didn't have to pay taxes?
In the prophet Ezra's time, King Artaxerxes made a law saying that priests, Levites, choir members, gate keepers, Temple attendants, and other workers in the Temple didn't have to pay taxes of any kind. (Ezra 7:24)

How did Joshua and his army make the walls of Jericho fall down?
God told Joshua that he and his army should walk around the city once a day for six days and then seven times on the seventh day. After they had done this, they were to blow their horns and shout. Joshua and his men did as God said. The walls of Jericho came tumbling down and the city was defeated. (Joshua 6)

What prophet was faster than a speeding horse?
Elijah. He outran King Ahab's chariot! (1 Kings 18:46)

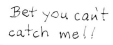

What city had itchy citizens?
Nineveh. All the people of the city wore sackcloth as a sign of asking forgiveness for their sins. (Sackcloth is *very* itchy!) (Jonah 3:6-9)

What "foxy" trick did Samson play on the Philistines?
He tied torches to the tails of foxes and let them loose in the Philistines' grain fields. All their crops were burned to the ground! (Judges 15:3-5)

THE MECHANICAL WORLD

What special talent did the men of the tribe of Benjamin have?

They were skilled at using slings in battle. David, who was a member of the tribe, killed Goliath with a sling when he was just a boy.
(1 Chronicles 12:2)

Where was the world's first piggy bank?

At the Temple in Jerusalem. Jehoiada, who was the High Priest at the Temple, placed a chest with a hole in the lid next to the altar at the Temple door. The offerings that people put into it were used to repair the Temple. (2 Kings 12:8-12)

What was Solomon's Laver (also called the Molten Sea)?

It was actually a giant washbowl that stood in the courtyard of Solomon's Temple. It was made of bronze and stood on the backs of 12 huge bronze oxen—and it held 54,000 litres of water! The temple priests washed their hands and feet in it. (1 Kings 7:23-26)

Why did Demetrius the silversmith start a riot in Ephesus?

The apostle Paul told people not to worship idols made of silver, which were popular in the city. Demetrius was losing business, and he and his fellow craftsmen were angry. (Acts 19:21-41)

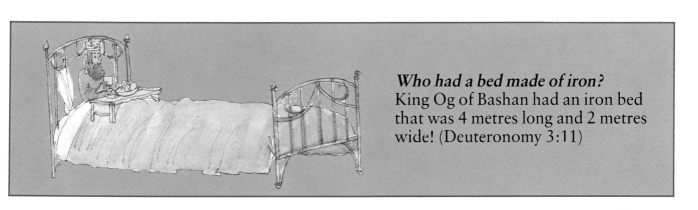

Who had a bed made of iron?

King Og of Bashan had an iron bed that was 4 metres long and 2 metres wide! (Deuteronomy 3:11)

What was Solomon's throne made of?

Solomon's huge throne was made of ivory and covered with pure gold. It had six steps, with a lion at either end of each step. (1 Kings 10:18-20)

What kind of hole did both Joseph and Jeremiah find themselves in?
They were both thrown into empty cisterns or wells—Joseph by his brothers and Jeremiah by four men who were afraid of his preaching. (Genesis 37:21-24, Jeremiah 38:6)

What did King Solomon own that was made of wood and had posts of silver, a canopy of gold, and purple seats?
His beautiful carriage—which he had built specially for him. (Song of Solomon 3:9-10)

What was special about the clothes and shoes the Israelites wore when they fled Egypt?
The Israelites wandered in the wilderness for 40 years. During that whole time, no one's clothes or shoes wore out! (Deuteronomy 29:5)

What did King Uzziah like to build?
Wells, and a lot of them, in the desert.
(2 Chronicles 26:10)

What structure did Haman build?
Haman had a 23-metre high gallows built when he planned to kill Mordecai. But Haman's plan backfired and it was he who was put to death on the gallows.
(Esther 5–7)

Daddy, why can't we live there?

Where did Jonadab want his descendants to live?
In tents. Jonadab told his family never to build houses, but always to live in tents.
(Jeremiah 35:6-7)

Well, well, well—what was one of the reasons Isaac had to move to Gerar Valley?
The Philistines were so jealous of Isaac's good crops and large flocks of animals that they filled all his wells with earth! (Genesis 26:12-15)

When is an uncut stone better than a cut stone?
When building an altar. The Law said that only uncut stones were to be used for building altars for worship and sacrifices. (Exodus 20:25)

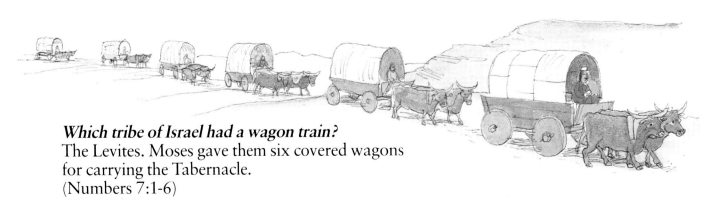

Which tribe of Israel had a wagon train?
The Levites. Moses gave them six covered wagons for carrying the Tabernacle. (Numbers 7:1-6)

What was Moses' antidote for a snakebite?
While in the desert, the Israelites complained against God, so he sent deadly snakes to punish them. Moses asked God to save the Israelites, so God directed Moses to make a bronze copy of a snake and put it up on a tall pole. All anyone who was bitten had to do to be saved was look at the bronze snake! (Numbers 21:4-9)

What did Aaron make for the frightened Israelites to worship while Moses was busy up on Mount Sinai?
Aaron made a golden calf —out of melted-down earrings! (Exodus 32:1-4)

Why did King Jehoshaphat of Judah build a fleet of ships?
He wanted his ships to go in search of riches like those that King Solomon's ships had brought back. But the fleet was destroyed before it set sail. (1 Kings 22:48)